WALKING

ON THE BEACHES
OF TEMPORAL CANDY

WALKING

ON THE BEACHES
OF TEMPORAL CANDY

CHRISTIAN
MCPHERSON

Walking on the Beaches of Temporal Candy

Copyright © 2020 Christian McPherson

Design by M. C. Joudrey and Matthew Stevens.
Layout by Matthew Stevens and M. C. Joudrey.

Published by At Bay Press October 2020.

All rights reserved. The use of any part of this publication, reproduced, transmitted in any form or by any means electronic, mechanical, photocopying, recording or otherwise, or stored in a retrieval system without prior written consent of the publisher or in the case of photocopying or other reprographic copying, license from the Canadian Copyright Licensing Agency-is an infringement of the copyright law.

No portion of this work may be reproduced without express written permission from At Bay Press.

Library and Archives Canada cataloguing in publication is available upon request.

ISBN 978-1-988168-40-1

Printed and bound in Canada.

This book is printed on acid free paper that is 100% recycled ancient forest friendly (100% post-consumer recycled).

First Edition

10 9 8 7 6 5 4 3 2 1

atbaypress.com

To those who go to a job every day but dream of something more.

B O O K 1

Poems Written While Travelling Around the Sun

Windless, Restless	3
Breathin	5
Mr. Silicon	7
Bubble Gum Bubble	9
Titanic	11
The New Magic	12
Daydreaming on a Bar Stool	14
The Heartbroken Tavern	15
If the Shoe Fits	17
Ms. Know-it-all	19
Cosmic Kiss	20
Temporal Candy	22
Mental Cramp	24
Monster Mind	26
The Implicit Understanding Between the Cashier and Me	28
After a Few Glasses of Wine, Admiring the Christmas Tree	30
I Open	31
Missing Logic	33
Thanks for Your Time	35
Wearing Ghosts	36
The Android	39

Laying Awake Beside My Sleeping Wife *41*

Trivial Knowledge *42*

Seasonal Affective Disorder *44*

The Origins of Swearing *45*

The Screamer *46*

My Neoclassical Babe *48*

Sometimes *50*

The Gooey Stuff *52*

'Till Death Do Us Part *54*

The Howl and Whistle *56*

Silly Game *58*

The View from the Top *60*

Mad Hatter *62*

A Failure of Successful Pieces *64*

The Commitment *66*

Likely Not Newsworthy *68*

Sunrise in Prince Edward County *69*

Time Travelers *71*

Transition to Autumn *73*

Those Cotton Candy Clouds *74*

Bench Pressing God *76*

Fixed Star Canopy *78*

Johnny Carson and the Universe *80*

Monkey Thoughts *82*

The Voices in My House *84*

Hopping into the Van, on Acid, with my Father to go
to McDonald's *85*

Thanksgiving *Novocaine* *87*

As the Crow Flies *89*

Everything for You *90*

This Forest a Theatre 92

Metamorphosis 94

Sunrise in Ottawa...95

Work Planner 96

The Homeless Man Standing on the Corner 97

Seagulls in the November Sky 102

Magic Window...105

Eating Peanuts 107

Incomprehensible 109

Dirty Sponge..111

Me, a Gift...113

The Clocksmith 114

The Beauty of the Woods 116

It All Washes Up on the Shore 117

A Love Poem for My Children 120

The End..122

BOOK 2

Poems Written on the Walk to Work

SPRING

Melt *131*

While You Were Sleeping *133*

Drunk on the Sun *135*

Pizza Box *137*

Copper Trees *139*

High in the Sky *141*

Bandaid Greetings *143*

Responsible Citizen *146*

Palpitations *148*

Sign: Large Lot for Sale *150*

Oz *151*

The Deep Sadness of the Sky *153*

Steamy Bus Streaks By *155*

Evolution *156*

Poor Visibility *158*

Adolescent lawn *160*

In Good Order *161*

Circles *163*

Machine Gun *165*

Shameful *166*

Comic Relief 167

My Giant Shadow 169

Spring Sprung 170

SUMMER

The First Day of Summer 177

Engaged with My Surroundings 179

War Machine 180

The Garden 183

Dress Code 185

The Secret Menu 187

The Shoe 188

An Ocean of Sky 190

Weeds 192

Steamy Hot Flesh 194

Empty Tree Branch Waits 196

As the Ash Trees Die 197

Walking to Work with My Dead Friend 199

Thought for Food 202

Empty Rum Mickey 203

Heat Wave 204

Melting Clouds 207

Dick and his Dog Spot 209

Pixelating Summer 210

What I Didn't Know 212

Crows Perched on Crosses 214

Equinox 215

AUTUMN

The Young Leaf Forgets..219

All the Leaves Dying..220

God's Halitosis 221

My Aunt Lost Her Sight..222

Dripping Faucet Sky...223

Hendrix Plays Dylan 224

The Banana Peel..225

My Sky a Teabag 226

Iridescent Leaf 227

I Walk Briskly Now..228

Profound Wet Sadness..229

A Dripping Faucet 230

Mailbox Graffiti 231

Walking Through Colour 232

The Wind Carries Me..233

Industrial Boots 234

Daylight Savings Time 235

Ideas Pour Out 236

The Grey Clouds Stab Me 237

Colour Power Punch...238

A Funny Tree Kicked..239

A Black Bare Oak Branch 240

It is This Moment..241

WINTER

Liquid Paper 245

The Snow 247

Dominatrix...249

Mr. Saggy Balls and Ms. Suicide 250

Cold Jazz 252

Bitch Slapping the Sky 254

It Keeps Him Out of Trouble 255

Extra Christmas Lights 257

The Existential Quandary of Rudolph 258

The Two Christmas Trees of Kilborn Avenue 259

Winter's Bony Hand...261

Lean Cuisine Wrapper 263

I Paint the City's Dreams 264

Walking in the Aftermath 267

Snow Eats Consciousness...269

Bedside Table 270

Ken Goes Surfing 272

I Flew Up in the Air and Landed on my Ass 273

The Escape Artist..275

Acknowledgments 277

B O
O K
1

Poems Written While Travelling Around the Sun

Windless, Restless

The park is still
windless
like somebody put it on pause

it is November
but the sun goofed
thought it was late September

three passenger jets
rake streaks of white clouds
into the ground of the sky

I push my son in the baby swing
even though he is four

I think
this may be the last time I do this

not such a bad thing

I try not to think about death
I try not to think about existence
and try to make some meaning
for my life

all these blades of grass

all these grains of sand
all for what?
just being here
pushing the swing

for my restless mind
it will have to do
at least
for today.

Breathing

I can make out the sound
of my son
across the hall
slight and shallow
like somebody labouring
very slowly
to inflate a bicycle tire

the dog in the living room
snorts like a dragon

and my daughter in the next room
beautifully silent
like a fashion magazine

my right nostril
is whistling Dixie

my wife is Darth Vader

I jostle the bed
and she rolls over
and switches to a mellow
Fred Flintstone

the furnace kicks on

and the house
begins to breathe
I lie very much
awake
listening
waiting
for
the
alarm
to suck all the air
out of the room.

Mr. Silicon

There is a man
who looks like me
      exactly like me
who lives on a different planet
in another galaxy

he drives his son to daycare
drops his daughter at school
goes to work
and pushes the buttons of logic
to realign cultural shock waves
to the chagrin of his motivation

he thinks absurd thoughts
they tumble *ad infinitum*
a jackass in a tractor tire
rolling down a hill

the winding of the machinery
the ticking pulse of the circuitry
the hum inside his head

a door on his forehead pops open
and a cuckoo bird springs free
on a mechanical metal arm
the little fellow belts out opera

and the man cries at the sound
of its beautiful voice
my twin writes his crazy thoughts
down

he writes a poem
and calls it
      Mr. Carbon.

Bubble Gum Bubble

My seven-year-old daughter
just came running
down the hall
crazed muppet arms and legs
screaming that she
just blew her first
bubble gum bubble

I remember the first bubble I blew
working that pink goo
like an old-school baseball pitcher
would work a wad of chewing tobacco

I was in the back seat of my parents' car
we were driving in Florida
when it came over the radio
Elvis was dead

I think my father may have cried
I remember him being sad
I didn't know who Elvis was
except he was a singer
and my father liked him

two days ago, they put Jack Layton
in the ground

my eyes spit on and off
like a kinked water hose
and my daughter has no idea
who he was

someday a kid that I won't know
will blow his first bubble gum bubble
and on that day my heart will stop
maybe someone will shed a tear
maybe not

so it goes.

Titanic

Navel orange
your belly

my lips'
captain

travels to the isle
of rib

steer my vessel to your mouth
and hit
an iceberg

slowly my ship
sinks
down.

The New Magic

This might be the last year
my kids believe in Santa Claus

I don't like lying to them
but then again
adulthood
like an unkempt fat man
stinking of ripe cheese
who gets into a crowded
elevator with you
seems far
far too close

my son told me
that a boy at school
told him
that the tooth fairy
was just his parents
I told my son
that was crazy
          how could that be?
thankfully he seemed to agree

when I finally saw
my parents
not as parents

12

but saw them
as people
trying to make it
in the world
it was like I found
the secret compartment
in the magic hat

and this revelation
was a new magic
for me
expectations lowered
back down
to human levels

I wonder how long
my super powers
will last

Daydreaming on a Bar Stool

Would her skin smell of soap?

would her armpits
taste of powder and sweat?

would her lips stink
of wine and cigarettes?

my nose in her hair
inhaling her scalp

would it be perfume
and oranges?

what's her flavour?

I'll never know.

The Heartbroken Tavern

In a leopard-skin jacket and sunglasses
Johnny Vegas asks the crowd
    the gyrating weeble-wobble dancers
    "What is better than one Frank Sinatra song?"
my friend who is standing beside me
at the bar says
    "He uses the same jokes over and over,"
and the crowd roars the answer in unison
    "Two Frank Sinatra songs!"

my friend tells me
"This is what happens to you
    when you get divorced
    and you are over 40."

my friend is ten years my senior
two divorces wiser
wears his sadness
like the moss ribbons
of an old oak tree

around the room
blue worms crawl
the knotted wood
through the desolation
of forest fire comb-overs

and liver-spot camouflage
chicken arms
wishbone-weak
she can still clutch a G&T
spin like Ginger R.
when a man half her age
asks her to dance

we watch the spectacle
as we finish our beers

over the loud music my friend yells
"So, you go home and tell your wife you love her,"

he means it

and that's exactly
what I do.

If the Shoe Fits. . .

Running through life
with banana peels
strapped to your feet
you learn about
pillows and duct tape
and speeding up
taking the turns
of fortune
tellers
marketing
my lifeline
out to the sea
big banana boat
sunscreen
we all screen
for sun screen
for cancer
ruling out
prognosis
not looking so
good on you
son

son
did anyone tell you
that you got

a strange sense
oh, a dime
toothpaste
a sixth sense
of humour?

son
did anyone tell you
if the shoe shits (*asshole pair*)
did anyone tell you
that you have
fruity shoes?

Ms. Know-it-all

She ate how-to books
        by the baker's dozen
wolfed down exercise videos
        like potato chips
gulped newspaper columns
        like bar shots
swallowed the internet
        whole
consumed art classes
        always chewed the still life
gobbled up self-help literature
        written by turkeys
munched on the aesthetician's handbook
        by the hairs of her chinny-chin-chin
sipped on psychology-lite
        and licked a few philosophy popsicles

she was full of advice

she asked me if I wanted some
she told me it was free
I told her you get what you pay for

I told her no thanks
I already ate.

Cosmic Kiss

There is a woman
who sits two hundred
billion light years away

she sits and thinks
about me
as I think
about her

her avocado
Star Trek skin
her sixties miniskirt
her tight red
V-neck sweater

she writes me a love letter
that I'll never read

I write her this poem
that she'll never see

we don't need to

her telepathy
my guesswork

a cosmic kiss

a comic kiss

in another life

star-crossed lovers.

Temporal Candy

It was the very
tiny tip
of the top
of a mountain

a few hundred million years later
a grain of sand

propelled by the surf
it tumbles forward
becomes part of the beach
indistinguishable from the rest

I step on it

down the beach
a turtle is struggling
on its back

my benevolent intellect
tosses the little fellow back
into the sea

as his little feet
kick away
the mountain peaks

rest below
on the bottom
of the ocean floor

in a few hundred million years
the grain of sand
might return to the top

I dance my dance
my Elvis waltz
my *Zorba the Greek* mambo
my *Saturday Night Fever* dance
of million coloured lights

I dance my dance
on the beaches
of temporal candy.

Mental Cramp

Lying on a beach
face pressed against your towel
you stare at the grains of sand
thinking of the history of the breakdown

organs, bones, veins
cells, molecules, atoms
protons, neutrons, electrons

now flavours of quarks
up, down, charm
strange, top, bottom

is it in here where the soul lies?
is this where consciousness
does its dance?

who's asking?
good question from the upper deck

memory being eaten like a burning piece of paper

who is asking?
or should it be why? or is that the same thing?

your silicon doppelganger from the parallel universe

does he not think the same thoughts as you,
you proud-to-be-alive carbon being?
puzzle solver, artist, the philosophy conman
how do you all measure up to the intellect of the house fly?

would you could you think any differently the next time?

no, you would do it the same
even if you would like to think otherwise.

Monster Mind

I've been doing the same work
for so long
that my frontal lobe
has a thick callus

I've tried to soften it
with alcohol
but it just dries it out
gets even harder

like the man
who complained for years
about having headaches
the x-ray revealing
a nail in his head

my PET scan
showed a troll
living in my brain
who is constantly
masturbating
and spraying obscene
graffiti on the inside
of my skull
        horrible things
        about my writing

about what a loser I am
       and why don't I just quit
       already?

the doctor said
such beasts are quite common
amongst artsy types

he prescribed Ativan
and sent me to a psychotherapist

I sit at my desk
rubbing my temples

headache? asks my co-worker

a little one
I answer.

The Implicit Understanding Between the Cashier and Me

And the kid at the cash looks at me
and I'm the next in line
and I look back at him
and there is this lightening understanding
and we are in this existential game together

and he is the guy who will ask me for my *Air Miles* card
and he is asking the old man in front of me for his *Air Miles* card
and when it's my turn he asks me
and then he asks me if I want a bag
and then he asks me how I'm going to pay
and he sees my bank card
and says "Debit?"
and I answer "Yeah"
and he hits a button on his cash
and says "Go ahead"
and I go ahead
and while I'm going ahead he bags my *Odor-Eaters* Insoles
and foot powder
        (my edge on my coworkers for advancement:
             the lack of any perceptible body odour
                "Hey, at least McPherson doesn't drool
                    or stink too badly")

and I open my bag
and the kid tears the receipt from the tiny jaws of the cash register
and stuffs the paper into the mouth of my plastic grouper
and he looks up at me
and we exchange another look
and it's the one that says we are almost done with this whole charade
and it's the one that acknowledges that we are both so human
and yet here we are playing the roles of customer and cashier
and how goddamn silly it is
and yet we must go on like this or society will burn to the ground
and I politely say "Thank you"
and he responds "Have a good day"
and what he really means is I know what you know
and you know what I know about everything we just faked here
and that's okay because we are keeping society from burning to the ground.

After a Few Glasses of Wine, Admiring the Christmas Tree

She's a damn beauty
this year
a fat triangle
plump like a belly dancer
coloured lights for her
the harlot
turning tricks
for the fat man
in the red suit
waiting for him
       (wobbly
       after he has consumed
       his eggnog and rum)
to stuff his gifts
into her green
undercarriage.

I Open

I open my eyes
and materialize back
into my life

I open the day
with ever increasingly
creaky bones
           cranky muscles

I open the tap
shower steam opens
my mind

I open the front door
and somebody has made
the world again

I open the newspaper

I open the coffee can
I open the drawer
I open the cupboard
I grab a bowl and spoon

I open the fridge
and realize

nobody bought milk

"Shit" I say
as
I close.

Missing Logic

The capacity for loss
or regret
or being capable
of missing something
of missing someone
makes no sense
if you are dead

you need a live brain
for that
(even if it's just in a vat)

to say I'll miss my kids
or miss the sound of crows
or the taste of your neck
when I'm gone
is ludicrous

I'll miss them just the same

I'll miss missing
I said it anyway
tossed it in the gears
of logic
and watched logic
gnash its teeth

logic won't miss me
but I'll miss it too.

Thanks for Your Time

A watch

that's what they're giving me
for fifteen years of service

a watch

a cliché

all the time I've given them

maybe it's their way of giving
time back to me

maybe I'll wear it to be inspirational
      look what you can get

maybe I'll throw it in the river

water resistant
up to thirty metres

a northern pike runs late.

Wearing Ghosts

Sitting in the park
I'm watching my son
slide down the plastic red slide
in his *Green Lantern* shoes
doing his best *Silver Surfer*
doing his best *Lords of Dogtown*
arms like airplane wings
       knees bent
        concentration and a smile
           sharing the spotlight

he jumps at the end
giving me his 8.9 landing

I smile
giving him applause

my daughter is
K2ing the blue bars
of the neighbouring structure
I give her the good job lingo

the clouds are
woven out of grey wool
they shake themselves
like a dog after a bath

and I pull up my jacket's hood
snap a few buttons together
it's a cheap nylon jacket
I've had it for close to twenty years
the zipper is busted
its utility long past retirement

it was my stepfather's jacket
he's been dead for over ten years
I wonder if his DNA lingers on it
I feel close to him when I wear it

in the winter
I wear my father-in-law's leather coat
he had it less than a year
before he passed away

I think of him almost
every time I put it on
        I wonder if my wife does the same

melancholy sewn into the fabric
I live in the skin of ghosts
bring them to life watching
their grandkids
        haunting the playground

the clouds up the ante

invoke a lawn sprinkler sensibility

I tell my children
it's time to go home.

The Android

His silicon cock swells
when he views the image
nipple, cunt, cherry cola
after all he was programmed that way

he has an affinity for old movies
likes Chaplin, Keaton, Abbot and Costello
likes watching the three moons of Kandor
likes the smell of seawater
after all he was programmed that way

his movements are smooth
and when he runs
he runs to the tempo of angels
he runs to the rhythm of microchips
after all he was programmed that way

he comes home after a hard day
cracks a beer
flips on the screen
and watches *The Stepford Wives*
cackles away while eating popcorn
while swilling back another beer
after all he was programmed that way

he writes poems about the light

coming through the window
in the late afternoon
on a lazy Sunday
and the loud thunder of silence
as the cat rests on the arm of the sofa
after all he was programmed that way

his tear ducts were well-built
the saline squirts from his eyes
his upper lip quivers
as he visits Alan Turing's grave
after all he was programmed that way.

Laying Awake Beside My Sleeping Wife

What is the point...

there is a door
        in my mind

fears lie on the other
                  side

cancer
suicide

maybe just marriage
        and a day job

that existential conundrum
        though
        has to be
            the worst thing

        that behind the door
                there is nothing

        nothing

            at all.

Trivial Knowledge

Sometime I become overwhelmed
by the futility of everything

how do I work my phone?
what command do I type?
which way does it go in?
how does an atomic clock work?
is there an app for it?
who won the hockey game?

learning how to operate the new microwave
so I can defrost chicken
knowing one day I will be old
and forget how the buttons worked
the microwave broken
sitting by the refuse
curbside

Mr. Boneless Skinless
how much time of my life
did I waste watching you spin
in the glow of the box?

no one will benefit
from my arcane knowledge

makes me want to put on boxing gloves
and get into the ring with philosophers
and punch a few out

I imagine the paramedic
placing the oxygen mask over my face
I mumble

>   thanks for studying
>   you're keeping my culinary prowess
>   alive
>   a little bit longer.

Seasonal Affective Disorder

The trees in my neighbourhood
have all come down
with a bad case
of autumn
and they have
puked their leaves
everywhere

I crunch by
these technicolor lawns
on my way to work
and it occurs to me
that maybe I'm coming down
with this illness too

I turn around
go home
and call in
sick.

The Origins of Swearing

On a stinking hot summer day
a six-foot-two man
with wide shoulders
got underneath a small
bathroom sink
with a dinky pair
of pliers
to change
20-year-old
rusted
plumbing

the bolt that wouldn't turn
the slipping
the mashing of knuckles
cuts to the hands
face

TURN, YOU FUCKING ASSHOLE !!!!!

and that's
how swearing came to be.

The Screamer

You find yourself
in your kitchen
your wife is screaming
your kids are screaming
the phone is screaming
the TV is screaming
the doorbell is screaming
the car alarm is screaming
the dogs are screaming
the radio is screaming
the nympho-neighbours are screaming
all the appliances are screaming
and you are
about to lose your mind
just trying to find
the end
of the
Saran
Wrap
and you run out the door screaming
and run to the bar
and order a double
and the game is on
and the fans are screaming
and the coach is screaming
and the ref is screaming

and the bartender is now screaming
at the TV
and the woman on her cellphone
is screaming
and you order another double
and you order another double
and soon you are screaming
and soon everything is screaming
the salt shaker is screaming
the toilet in the men's room is screaming
the chewing gum stuck to the underside of the table is screaming
and you are now staggering down the street
the ambulances go by screaming
and you finally get home
and you are refrigerator spelunking
compiling an extra pickle grand slam
which you nickname 'The Screamer'
which would be on the menu
of your imaginary restaurant
which you plot as you chew your food

your wife silently comes into the kitchen
and quietly asks if you are coming to bed
and you nod
without a sound.

My Neoclassical Babe

I awoke
and opened
my eyes
to a true vision
of beauty
Flaming June
sleeping
right beside
me

I thought
how can this
girl
be here
in my bed?

how did I
get so
lucky?

then she stirred
and opened
her eyes
a little

I said

"You're beautiful"

"I'm not having
sex, I'm still tired"

"No really, I just
meant you're
beautiful"

"Thanks, you're sweet"

my neoclassical
painting
rolled over
and went
back to sleep.

Sometimes

Sometimes I just want to wrap my arms
around the world
and squeeze with all my might
because it's all so fucking fragile
because it's all so
finite

sometimes I want to walk up to complete
strangers
and hug them
because I know they are going to die

sometimes I lie in my bed and pretend
I'm lying in a coffin
the world going on above me
people running in muted thumping shoes
like I were sitting on the bottom
of a swimming pool
       the muffled laughter of children
       playing tag on my grave

sometimes I want it with fries
sometimes I want to grab a stick
of *Juicy Fruit*
sometimes I want to punch the loud guy
in the corner

in the mouth
sometimes I want to taste the beauty
of your skin
sometimes I want nothing

sometimes I just want more sometimes

sometimes.

The Gooey Stuff

My son came into the room
asked me what I was watchin'
I told him it was a documentary
about consciousness
about what some people think
about what happens when you die

I could see he was thinking about it

later
walking the dogs together
we began to talk about it again

I told him what I thought
I told him I thought
your brain is like a computer
except instead of metal and silicon
we are tissue, blood, DNA, and all that gooey stuff

I said when you die
it's like turning off the computer at home
except you can't turn it back on

I could see he was thinking about it

it's what the gooey stuff does

think about it

we walked the dogs
    and I thought about the implications
    of my analogy
    for morality
        responsibility and legal consequences

we walked and talked
and quickly the conversation moved to video games
and hockey
    after all he is nine

the next thing we knew
we were home
before our gooey stuff
could give it much more thought.

'Till Death Do Us Part

My wife and I watch *Dateline*
on Friday nights

the program often
focuses on a murder

usually it's about one spouse
killing the other

Keith Morrison spins the tales
with a creaky spidery voice
about jealousy and betrayal
lies and deceit
in the bedrooms of America

a fleshy new boyfriend
shoots an old wrinkled husband

the wife goes all Agatha Christie
and just disappears

windshield wiper fluid
antifreeze
cyanide

my wife brings me a fresh drink

during the commercial

I take a sip
letting my tongue hunt
for the taste of bitter almonds
or a sickly aftertaste

it tastes completely normal

"Thanks for the beer," I say

"Just don't ever cheat on me," she says
giving me her best Edgar Allan Poe stare

the sepia image of a blood stain reappears
on the TV
and we are happy.

The Howl and Whistle

I'm in bed
sick
reading a novel
about a failed love

a spring rain
and a howling wind
outside my window
like an angry lover
bursting into a room
spitting and hurling
words
that later
would be as cast
in unforgiving stone

the window behind me
is open a tiny crack
and it's whistling and howling
like a shrieking child
like a wounded animal in pain
and then it sounds
like the screaming of young lovers

it makes me think
about the cruelty of the world

an animal caught in a trap,
the way she looked at him
at the dinner party

I listen to the fight
like they were apartment neighbours
knowing
the whole time
it's really
only the wind.

Silly Game

My daughter and I
are zigzagging our
way through the school
playground

we are doing the landmine shuffle
the war movie tripwire tango
the Scooby Doo booby-trap bounce
the Ninja hot foot hop

we are avoiding
all the lines
            marking the ground
            like an LSD spider web

the yellow painted calculator
hopscotch squares
cement fissures

I accidently step on a crack
and just like that
my daughter tells me
in her unconditional referee voice
            I'm out

and somewhere in the world

a mother has been in a horrible collision
> fractures to her T12 and L1 vertebrae

I take no responsibility.

The View from the Top

Driving down the road
I see it standing there
looking like a giant version
of a child's medieval
shoebox castle

I remember looking out the window
of his room
over the trees and houses below

it was June and the leaves
had come in full
everything green
full of life

I remember thinking
it's a nice enough view

it can't be sunsets
and rainbows all the time
now can it?

I drive by
the hospital where my stepfather
passed away
and think about

all the people
in those rooms up there
think about
their view from the top

it's a nice enough view
yes
for your last one,
it will do just fine.

Mad Hatter

I'm sitting in a giant teacup
my daughter is across from me
a metal table between us
her smile is ridiculously happy
and in that moment
I hope my last thought on earth
will be that smile

Johnny Depp stares at us
from the placard
as we go spinning by
mushrooms
and Alice
and the carny
       with a *Brillo* pad stash
       grey ringlets like a Renaissance wig
       bungee-cording down past his chin

Strawberry Fields is playing
       with auditory baseball-
       bat-to-the-head-volume
as our saucer lifts off
       tossing us into the air
       a garden-party stumble

my daughter closes her eyes

but her smile remains crazyglued
>	I'm hoping the bolts remain tight
>	hoping the cinnamon mini doughnuts
>	remain
>	in my belly

when it's done
skipping off the electric ghost of Lewis Carroll
we meet my wife and my son
>	he comes running
>	with a six-foot blue
>	made-in-China snake
>	Tarzaned around his body
>	a bursting balloon smile

>	the other image I ring-toss into my brain

we all wander off
in search of something.

A Failure of Successful Pieces

You listen to the music of your youth
nostalgia bubbling in your head
like *Alka-Seltzer* tablets
    everything was so last-second-of-the-game
    important like French fashion models
    desire and love were musical chairs
    lost by friends
    won by enemies

and the lab-coat boys
turned on their ray guns,
and zapped your incredible life
shrinking it down to a manageable size
for your ego to digest

seeing the dots
connecting them as a gypsy fortune teller would
bunching them tight as astrology
you move forward
no longer hopping the fence
but walking around it

the writing is more important than ever
and yet
it feels like a series of pieces
a failure of successful pieces

a smashed china plate
mosaic

beautiful

broken.

The Commitment

When you light a cigar
you make a commitment
to the stained hands
the knotted knuckle flesh
of the factory worker
who rolls the tobacco leaves
in the factories of Havana

       marine lead paint
       flakes from the walls
       as a boy runs by
       the open door
       hoop and stick
       his sidecar

when you light a cigar
you make a commitment
to your bottle of Scotch
and a commitment to your friend
to discuss the most important matters
of the world at hand

       (a sale on toothpaste
       corrupt literary judges
       the war on Trevor)
       Freud knew this to be true
       as did Churchill
       and Capone

when you light a cigar
you make a commitment
to the beauty of the night
to the birds of sundown
and the bats of dusk

when you light a cigar
you make a commitment
to smoke it
right down
to the
nub.

Likely Not Newsworthy

With the summer
almost on empty
I walked to work
and out from behind
a big apartment building
            popped
two hot air balloons
with advertising across
their warm bellies
CTV and The SUN

with dragon breath
and the laziness of clouds
they drifted over my head

I thought about
the people riding up in the sky
and then the thought
floated away too.

Sunrise in Prince Edward County

I awake to Mother Nature
gushing from her loins

a blood red orange
hangs in the sky
menstruating across the horizon
bleeding into the clouds

it's glorious
its magnitude amplified
by the silence
of the house
we rented in the countryside

I think about
waking my wife
but she is so tired
from the drive

and so I don't
and then I go back to
to my clandestine affair
with the pornographic sky
until her colours
run dry

I try to go back to sleep
but her fiery lips
and pink cumulous

are stuck
in my head

I get up
and the day has begun.

Time Travelers

Oil rings on the asphalt
peacock feather piss
a trapdoor portal
for time travelling
wide eyed
full pupil
experimenters of youth

I'm eating breakfast
beside these teleporters
beside these space cases
kids half my age
one young lad using the table
as a pillow
a pretty girl with a dishevelled aura
updates her Facebook timeline
with wireless technology

I would come here
to this restaurant
in worse shape
half assimilated
when I was their age

my wife and I
rarely pull out the space suits

rejoice we made it past
midnight with a PVR'd movie
the kids get up
and jetlag stumble
towards the exit
as our food arrives

now I cut my son's pancakes
~~after~~ spreading butter
before pouring maple syrup
and marvel at who I once was

it seems like only moments ago.

Transition to Autumn

The wind is angry
the trees are angry
from getting pushed around
soon they will turn red with anger
and the leaves will leave

I sit in my screened-in porch
sip my beer
and listen to my harmonica windows
air moving through them
the breath of a mean kid
blowing out
the candles of summer

this is when melancholy
grabs me around the chest
and the weather makes me
grab something fuzzy
to pull over my head

my wife says to me
"I wish my father hadn't died"

I understand
the wind blows so cold
and mean
I tell her
"me too."

Those Cotton Candy Clouds

I'm walking my two dogs
with my kids
and the clouds
have turned into
pink cotton candy
the sky
70s album cover art

I'm thinking about
this miracle of consciousness
100 billion neurons
and you get to experience
what I'm experiencing
a creature
that self-reflects

one of my dogs loses his mind
whenever large vehicles
or buses go storming by
his front paws moving
as if he's on a treadmill

me, taut as a sail in strong wind
holding him in place
he barks like he wants
the garbage truck to die

he does this because
that's the way he's programmed

I think about my thinking
because that's the way
I'm programmed

my daughter asks me
why does it take two years
to get to Mars?
I tell her
it's because it's
so far away
I tell her
maybe one day
she will go

I will never leave here
a prisoner
of my body
of the earth

stuck here
with the rest of you
inmates
lifers
watching
those cotton candy clouds.

Bench Pressing God

My capacity
is limited
my organic machinery
fallible
            a hole in my bag of walnuts
I dribble memories

            why am I looking
            inside this cupboard?

I can forget
to pick up milk
my dry cleaning
forget my own name
and yet
I can never
forget you
hardwired
into my cerebellum
like the guts of a pumpkin

I don't need tombstones
or holiday reminders
but the notes of a song
they can bench press God
project you sitting on my kitchen counter

smoking a cigarette
giving me a smirk
I play the song again
and have you back
just for another few
muscle memory
miracle minutes.

Fixed Star Canopy

If somebody put thoughts in my head
I wouldn't know it

if I were a brain
in a pickle jar
I couldn't tell

if the earth
were moving at
67,000 miles per hour
I wouldn't feel it

if you were to read this
now
or when I'm gone
I won't know

I know I put a thought
in your head

I doubt you are in a jar

I know the earth is moving

and we have shared this together
over time and space

maybe we do this under the
movement of Plato's fixed star canopy
on a warm summer night

that would be lovely
this I know.

Johnny Carson and the Universe

I think about of the death of Johnny Carson
and how he never spoke to Joan Rivers again
after she got her own show

I think about Ed McMahon's laugh
and my grandparents watching in bed
on a *Zenith*

I think of the baby boomers
how their generation is sunsetting
how the memory of Johnny Carson
will soon be lost

I think about a man in the South of France
who makes excellent wine
and spends his Sunday mornings
smoking cigarettes and drinking espresso

I've never met this man
I made him up
but I'm sure he exists

I never met Johnny Carson

I think of the death of my kids
I think of the death of my great-great-great grandkids

the ones I'll never meet
but hope they exist
I hope they exist

I'll reach out to them here and now
crossing time and space
      my memory
           message in a bottle
              nice to meet you

I think about the decay of everything
the finality of everything
I accept it
but I'm not entirely happy about it

existential rebel
I flip the universe the bird.

Monkey Thoughts

Get out your monkeys and typewriters
haven't we heard it all before?

how many monkeys
and how much time is required
to type out this poem?

the playful approach
the seriousness of the question
the frustration in it looping
pointing finger

what are the odds that we got here?

how many billions of years
did it take for Shakespeare to show up?
how many until he and Nietzsche
show up again?

the finite in the infinite
always coming back to that
never coming back
the monkeys may never have
any luck

humans lucky to have

their five minutes on
the cosmic clock
I wander to the kitchen
get a banana
snap its head
peel its yellow skin
bite into its white flesh

I wander back to my keyboard
marvel that I'm here
and begin to type again.

The Voices in My House

My wife gets mad sometimes
that everything in our house
has a voice
has a personality

"Try living with Robin Williams,"
says the salt shaker sarcastically

my wife leaves the room

"What's her problem?" I ask
as the voice of the pepper

"Maybe she felt assaulted?"
replies the salt

"Achoo," sneezes the pepper

the salt giggles.

Hopping into the Van, on Acid, with my Father to go to McDonald's

My father asked me
if I had been smoking dope
I was about eighteen
a mop of hair like a mop

I had been so grooving with my Beatles tape
turning it way up
because I knew he didn't care for
a lot of my "so-called" music
but I knew he liked them

"No, of course not," I told him honestly
he didn't seem impressed with me
I didn't care
I went with him because I found myself starving
coming down off the clouds

to my surprise
I found myself loving him
so much that day
the way he drove
the way his hair looked
so fantastic
so much love in my heart

and my *Quarter Pounder*™ with cheese
when I bit into that sucker
it was fucking God.

Thanksgiving *Novocaine*

I can see things
see myself pulling the bird
from the oven
its golden crisp skin
beautiful
delicious

and with very little
in the way of luck
this is how it will be

my daughter
mixes breadcrumbs
with sage
translucent onions
tender celery

after I make the dead bird dance
after I'm told I'm silly
her smile like *Novocaine* against time
I get her to roll up her sleeves
high past the elbow
get her to stuff

we tie a piece of string
necrophilia bondage

around its legs
to keep it all locked inside
as it cooks
I work on potatoes
and carrots
and think about
the future
driving lessons
moving boxes
all the things I will do
in my life

the talk of the journey
not the destination
I understand now
it's about the *Novocaine*

my end
I will never see it coming
some inane last thought
        (*should have taken out the garbage*)

I see how it will end
        poorly

I open the oven door
and there is my bird
perfect.

As the Crow Flies

The crows fly by my crescent moon of October
as I pedal my bicycle
in the opposite direction
to work

clearly I'm going the wrong way.

Everything for You

When I see a blank page
I want to fill it with beautiful words
exquisite words like exquisite
I want to paint you a picture
of a mountain valley
with only these words
and when you read them
your mouth will fill with warm honey
and then peppermint
and then orange
and you will smell the words
of cinnamon
of oil rags
and gas cans

a flock of geese
an alarm clock
the gurgle of the coffee maker
the intense volume of silence

I want to give you everything
want to give it all to you

I stroke your flesh with these words
and you quiver and shake in your loins

I want to bring back your memories
and create a future we can share
listen now as I create an entire world
just for you.

This Forest a Theatre

This forest
where I walk my dogs
is a children's fairy-tale
in the winter

in the spring
it is a swamp
where two escaped prisoners
chained at the ankles
run from a pack of hounds

at night it's always Hallowe'en
despite the season

in the summer
it turns into
a humid mosquito-infested
Vietnam war film

and now autumn
the trees licorice
blackened wet
from the rain
the leaves fluorescent
iridescent lime
on the cusp of dying

such a spectacular way
to finish.

Metamorphosis

These poems
they take
a little bit out of me
a little blood spilt on the page
each time

I write them
and I write them

the pile gets bigger
and I get smaller

soon there will be
a stack of books
and beside them
nothing but an empty pen
and a pile of old clothes.

Sunrise in Ottawa

Walking to work
God smashed a creamsicle
       into the horizon
       painted the rest of the sky with blueberry ice
cream

I pass by squirrels
       flattened into burnt fuzzy pancakes on the road

       a crow picks at one

lights come on in the large grey buildings

a plane is ascending into the sky

by the time I get to my office
       the sky has melted back into grey November

the city is almost awake.

Work Planner

I have a black book
on my desk
at work

I use it to record
my daily work
at work

it looks like a bible

another reason
I'm an atheist.

The Homeless Man Standing on the Corner

He stands on the corner
at a city intersection
and holds his arms out
like crucified Christ
like a super hero about to fly off
when electricity suddenly pours from his finger tips
slithering fishers of light
Ghostbuster bolts of energy
Doctor Strange power blasts

this lightning cuts the air
wraps around the building
in front of the homeless man

these glowing streaks of magic
pick up people
lift them off the ground
float them in the air
put them in
        a Glenda Good Witch of the North stasis
where slack-jawed old ladies
and old men
watch their hats
and their fluffy little dogs float about them
their arms and legs stirring the ether
like they were floating in pancake batter

the icy white light
picks up children
and their parents
and the man in the turban
and the woman in the burka
and the dude slinging dope
and the banker slinging his briefcase
and the lady issuing a parking ticket
and all the rest of them who are rushing
about the block
about their day

the homeless man
lifts them all high into the air
like Magneto
a conductor

all street traffic stops
windows of cars go down
windows of surrounding buildings go up

everyone's eyes LSD-wide

the ring of light
the size of a city block
floating all those people in the air
radiates out
zapping all onlookers

hundreds of people
connected by the radiant umbilical cord
of the homeless man's fiery hands

then it happens
in a microsecond
everyone who is touched by the light
sees
        everyone else
knows
        every thought
of
        every person
of
        every living thing

the musician knows the schedule
        of the librarian
        who understands the Hindu's concept of God
        who knows about the surprise birthday party
        that was thrown for the 81-year-old lady
        (the one slowly spinning counter clockwise in the light)
        on her 50th birthday by her long-deceased husband
        the party she thinks about often
        the one that comforts her when she is lonely

a matrix of interconnected thoughts
a ubiquitous consciousness of understanding
a collective mind-meld of knowledge
a DMT-like brain orgy
enlightenment

and for a second
there is only love
       and the purest form of awareness
       that each and every thing
       accepts the presence of each
       and every other thing

and it lasts for just a second
then the homeless man puts everyone down
puts everything back with a wave of his hand
and immediately everyone
       forgets
everything that just happened
       like nothing happened

and the street scene resumes
the little old lady continues to walk her dog
the bylaw officer slips the ticket under the window
and the librarian drops her books
but the homeless man knows
they now all carry a tiny kernel
a microscopic seed

in their hearts
in their brains

he knows he has implanted them
        with love and understanding
        with empathy and kindness
        he knows he has changed them
even if it's so small you can't see it
even if it's so small you can't tell

he knows the kindness will come out
every once in a while
like a pimple

I pass by the homeless man
with his arms out

most people think he is crazy
but I know what he is really doing.

Seagulls in the November Sky

They fly about me
like I was inside
Dorothy's house
looking out the window
on the way to OZ
as I cross the empty
dirty
parking lot
of the shopping mall

gum wrappers
and cellophane
litter the asphalt

the cups of McDonalds
and Tim Hortons
lie squished
by the monsters
of Michelin
and Goodyear

a heap of cigarette butts
laze on a painted yellow line
of parking
where they were dumped
from the ashtray of someone's car

she needed to make room
for more

I notice the lipstick stains
on them

they match
the pink sunrise

I like to think
she wore a tight black miniskirt
and drove a Trans Am

likely an old woman
in sweatpants
in a K-car

inside the mall
the temperature
is contrastingly warm

there is Christmas music playing
and a tower of fake presents
climbing high into the sky
flanking Santa's empty seat

metal lattice covers store fronts
an old man walks with ski poles

and the escalators move
with nobody on them

the mall will be open
in a few hours

outside
the seagulls will be there
waiting for the shoppers
to arrive

outside in the November sky
the seagulls will be there
waiting
to shit on their cars.

Magic Window

I have a framed picture
a reproduction of
Lawren Harris'
Maligne Lake in Jasper Park
hanging on my cubicle wall

I often look at it
as if I were looking
out of an open window

I stare across the water
stare at the snow-capped mountains
and imagine the cold crisp air
filling my lungs
filling them with hope

the picture was given to me
by a colleague
when he retired

he told me
it got him through
thirty years

I stand on the shore
listening to the silence

while watching
the majestic sky

I am free.

Eating Peanuts

I'm standing in my kitchen
snapping and cracking
peanuts
tossing the shells
into the beige organic refuse container
located next to the sink

I think about the hundreds of millions of years
which came before me
on our little planet
I think about how very short my life is

it strikes me with terror
        but as quick as a shooting star
        the feeling flies away

I squeeze a nut
from its brown skin
it pops like a zit
bullets into my palm
into my mouth like medicine

I eat my peanut
with awe
it is the very fact I'm here
        eating a peanut

it's fantastic
like I suddenly got a second chance
at life

I think about the hundred million years
to come after I'm gone

I crack another shell
even though I think
I'm full.

Incomprehensible

Last summer
I shoveled a lot of gravel
turning my backyard into Disneyland

from this and the summer jobs of my youth
I know how heavy
rock and dirt and cement are

carry buckets of water a few blocks
and you'll know the weight of water

standing before the ocean
on my little section of beach
on my little section of the world
I find it difficult to comprehend
the mass of the earth
I find it difficult to truly understand
how big
        the world really is

and yet I've seen the Earth
from space
        not so big from up there

I know
because Google told me

that the Sun is so big
it can hold
one million and three
                    hundred thousand Earths

to feel the numbers
to give cognition to your heart
is impossible

when I read about the three children
and their grandfather removed from this big world
by a drunk driver

or when I read about the twin brothers
who died goofing around on a bobsled

or when I read about the Syrian father
whose family drowned
trying to escape the war

I try to understand
the grief of these parents

it's similar
to trying to understand how big
the universe is.

Dirty Sponge

Walking through the world
absorbing pop-culture like a sponge
every morning I hop in the shower
and scrub my skin
the pages of *People* magazine
and *Entertainment Weekly*
peel away
clogging my drain

free market choice
occupies my refrigerator
Kellogg's stains my throat
President's Choice my teeth
Colgate whitens with a body of evidence

my wireless technology informs me
about new wireless technology
which is going to pull my strings
and make my joy dance like a marionette

I work all day on a computer
making computer applications
so people can work all day
on a computer

my lunch is a neon box

on a plastic tray
of world cuisine
I purchase the *United Nations Club*
and taste the freedom
of mayonnaise filling my mouth

I glide with the efficiency
of escalators
into the den of consumption
into the storm of sovereignty
feeling the effects of emoticons
and boneless chicken
I know with the certainty of a discount
that I'm ~~truly~~ living the dream.

Me, a Gift

It's vampire dark outside
and the clouds have descended
swooped down like they were mopping up
a spilt drink

I walk through this
foggy soggy
mid-December

reindeer made of plastic
and metal
and lights
blink and flash
like runway lights
Rudolph's nose
guiding me down the road
delivering my body
to my employer

Christmas has come early
I remove my coat
rip it off like wrapping paper
sit in my office chair
and turn on my computer

I'm the shiny robot under the tree.

The Clocksmith

There is a man
who lives down the block

he's holocaust-
                    thin

I see him often outside
smoking
in his laneway

he moves with the speed
of the hour hand

he used to be a clocksmith
knows the tick and pulse
of micro- machinery

he told me
when he dies
all his knowledge
about how to fix
these winding
clocks
will
die
too

I think about his lungs
and guts
seizing up
hardening like clay
every time he inhales

somewhere
sometime soon
a grandfather clock
will chime for the last time.

The Beauty of the Woods

Never worry about me
for I know the beauty of the woods

*the woods are
lovely, dark,
and deep*

winter has come
and laid the white ash of frozen water
on every branch and twig

my lungs burn hot
with the cold air
as my nostrils steam
like a dragon

my boots crunch out
soft compressions
in the silence
which has dropped
like an atomic bomb

you can never feel sad
for anyone
who has known this
blazing frozen wood

it's where the soul quickly goes
quiet
and even atheists
        think of God.

It All Washes Up on the Shore

Walking along the beach
where the surf crashes
feet from my feet
frothing my toes
with milky salt water
I watch the tide
wash ashore
pieces of my life

the old oil furnace
from my childhood basement
the one that gave me the heebie jeebies

Lego bricks tumble
like brightly-coloured
pieces of coral

further down
my Commodore Vic 20
and my Atari gaming system
get dumped before me

up ahead
I see my teenaged
beer bottle collection
bobbing like brown jellyfish

condoms
packs of cigarettes
and philosophy books
come spinning ashore
as I continue
down the beach

old roommate couches
and cheap Ikea furniture
beached like whales

further ahead
I can see my daughter's soother
and my son's crib

and can't see where
the beach ends
or where the objects
stop washing up

but this is where I stop
remove all my clothes
and dive into the ocean

I swim out until
I cannot touch
and here I float
and listen to the surf

endlessly
crash.

A Love Poem for My Children

My arms aren't big enough
                    strong enough
to hug you for an eternity
and I know one day
I will have to let go
so you
can be
you

always know this
I carry you with me
in each beat of my heart
until it beats no more
then you can carry me
in your heart
until it beats no more

and when we are both gone
always know this
there was so much
            LOVE
that at times it overwhelmed me
there was so much
            LOVE
a volcano spitting
            double rainbows of butterflies and bonbons

it was a knife to cut through
the insignificant blather
the meaningless sales pitch
the flashy expense

it was crepes and syrup Sunday mornings
popcorn cuddles
and thumb war laughter

it was secret handshakes
living room theatre
and underdogging the swing

the love
now this
a memento
always.

The End

Give it to me straight:

how long do I have Doc?

how long is this movie?

how long to we have to go?

how long is the wait?

how long have you been waiting?

how long is the line?

shoe tapping

pull out the phone

blow hair off your face with an upturned extended lip
like a whale spout
           pout

more shoe tapping

and SNAP
           just like that

the end arrives
so quick

you almost didn't see it coming.

BOOK 2

Poems Written on the Walk to Work

The world wants you to work the lawn or walk the dog or paint the house - anything but write, just so you bleed whatever energy you have away from writing, and if you're not careful that's exactly what you're going to end up doing.

Harry Crews

SPRING

a bee kissing a blossom

Melt

It all pulls back
uncovering what we lost

the deposits of gravel
turning melting snowbanks
poppy seed

everyone walking around
all post traumatic
shaking their heads
muttering
that they can't believe it
that they survived
another winter

you said
you didn't want
any heroics
just let you go

but at the last second
you said yes
to the stomach tube
kept the suffering
chugging along
a little longer

to finally let go
let it all melt away
turning it all to tears
then vapour
well that's hard as glacial ice.

While You Were Sleeping

While you were sleeping
I wrestled the alarm clock
and lost

I pulled the rip cord
on the coffee maker
and assembled the future
in the form of packed lunches

I closed the door softly
so as to not wake you
and found the world lovely
yet again

while you were sleeping
I absorbed my surroundings
and then used telepathy
like a comic book superhero
to send all this magic
to your dreams
so they were smeared with the vitality
of Spring

while you were sleeping
I sent elves
in a golden carriage

pulled by unicorns
with bouquets of tulips
and baskets of peppermint candies
I sent them to your subconscious
so when you awoke
beauty and kindness would linger on your
fingertips and tongue
like morning dew
and the world would seem like
it had been given a fresh coat of paint
a haircut
and new shoes

while you were sleeping
all the way to work
I thought about
you.

Drunk on the Sun

The sun
a golden fist
punching a hole
into the pale blue pool-liner
of my suburban sky

drivers race towards it
sun visors down
sunglasses on
and their eyes still water
like their corneas
swallowed chili peppers

my shadow
a giant
I drink the sun
like my stomach was made
of solar panels
my blood
      battery acid
my brain
      a cactus

I drink the sun
until I'm
drunk on it

dehydrated
staggering through the desert
I drink the sun
until
I have
a feeling
there is hope
for humanity.

Pizza Box

Someone has taken a trowel
and smoothed out the clouds
into wet grey plaster

the seagulls fly
under the fresco sky

and my thoughts
are scrambled Easter eggs
soaking into the canvas
jumping and spring boarding
from full hop
        to non sequitur

maybe too much beer last night?
maybe not enough coffee this morning?

I pass the house
where I found the cell phone
the one I returned
when its owner called

I didn't feel right
        about leaving it in the street

he was a young man

late twenties
early thirties
Japanese motorcycle
and a pickup truck in the driveway

after he thanked me
I drove home on my wife's beige electric scooter
with the big flower on the side

I haven't seen his truck all winter

did he move?
did he forget to make the payments?
lose his licence?

the clouds suck my thoughts like a sponge

the empty pizza box in the driveway
with all its implications
connotations
two a.m. debauchery

like I would know
anything about that.

Copper Trees

Birds are singing

one sounds like
a garden sprinkler
on its fast return

the ghost of a skunk
creeps the air

they're knocking
down little houses
and putting up
tidal waves of bricks
and glass
and opulence

in the middle of a block
there is a shiny new house
decorated
with four cedar bushes
five feet tall
shaped like candyfloss tops
shaped like perfect plastic
LEGO trees

last year's drought

killed the bottom
three shrubs
they stand there
dead
next to their
live
green sister
looking like they were made of copper

if the owners had watered them
just once
they might have lived

but they didn't
and their Audi still fits
nicely into the garage.

High in the Sky

A crow sits on the arm of a cross
on the tower of church
like one of those men
eating lunch
building the Empire State

the clouds are rolled up high
bunched at the top
like a window blind

a Canadian flag droops
like a wilted cock
on the roof of a government tower

somebody somewhere
                on a balcony
                            thinking about it
                                stay or

                                        g
                                        o
                                        ?

you remain the ship run ashore
the bad child
the pilot of bad weather
of sound mind and body

you

remain

very

much

grounded.

Bandaid Greetings

Here comes the woman
walking up the hill
holding her young daughter's hand

they walk slowly
like the hill was Everest

they live in the apartment building
across the street
from where I work

it's an old building
lots of immigrants
lots of police cars

when I was a kid
my friend lived there
with his grandmother
because his parents died

the building was rough then
dope heads and welfare kings
      time hasn't softened it

the woman I see everyday
rarely looks at me

rarely makes eye contact
when she does
it affords me the opportunity
to say good morning

it strikes me
she might be distrustful of men
            maybe he struck her

I say good morning
trying to put a bandaid
on the gushing wound
left by my gender

she doesn't say anything
gives me the smallest of acknowledgments
with the tiniest upturn of her mouth

maybe I got it all wrong
maybe it's not that way at all

but she and her daughter
still live in the shitty building
and my salutations
can't fix that

the clouds
are about to

combat the earth

I feel a drop of rain.

Responsible Citizen

Today makes me want to
become manic depressive
throw away my meds
and lose my shit

today makes me want to
run around and steal convertibles
drive them with the top down
drive them to the casino
gamble away my life savings
jack up my credit cards
with hookers and cocaine
and then like W.C. Fields
                 waste the rest

today has crazy energy
the birds have been shooting
Walt Disney smack all night
and are performing princess songs
for some sort of world record

each step I take
I can feel the earth's vigour
surging into my body

I'm a piano on fire

and Jerry Lee is playing
the devil's music
the good-time twirl
of the jiving short skirt
flash of ass
I'm so ridiculously alive

then I get to work
a needle in the neck
a walloping dose of *Thorazine*

I sit at my desk
like McMurphy post electroshock

I look out my window

and drool on my shoe.

Palpitations

I'm up later than normal
and traffic
has already reached adolescence

I'm to be tested

I arrive at the other building
beside the shitty one
and ride the elevator to the fifth
where I don't plead
but wait in a room
until a woman enters
and orders me
to take off
my shirt

she applies alcohol
and suction cups
to my chest

24 hours
to monitor the rhythms
of my heart

will they find you in there
a mini you

working the arteries
      and pipes
      like the Wizard?

will they find my children
      playing tag
      sliding down my carotid?

will they find
a group of other women
lost loves
having a picnic on my left ventricle?

after I'm all Matrixed up
I dash across the street to work

I listen to my own footsteps
I listen to the sounds of the world

I cannot hear the sound
of my own heartbeat.

Sign: LARGE LOT FOR SALE

BUILD YOUR CUSTOM HOME RIGHT HERE

CALL THIS NUMBER NOW

Oz

The maple trees
are dropping
a fine lime flower pollen
which coats the sidewalks
like a Dayglo magic carpet

it's the closest thing I'll get
to a yellow brick road

it leads me
not to the Emerald City
but to a beige shopping mall

the parking lot is strewn
with fast food garbage
and gulls and crows
and the occasional deranged duck
fighting over french-fry wrappers

I enter the mall
away from rainbows
away from colour
to the black and white
world of computer binary

in my cubicle

at my desk

I click my heels together
three times

nothing happens.

The Deep Sadness of the Sky

The clouds are grey mold
creeping across
the Danish blue cheese atmosphere
closing the curtains
on the sun

the day
a cold damp basement
penicillin lactation imminent
the air filled with remorse
regret

did I tell you
I love you
enough?

did I tell you
how much
fun
I had?

I wear the weather
like a coat
it soaks into my skin
into my bones
and makes me

want to turn around
and run home
to you.

Steamy bus streaks by
folks enjoying a sauna
on the way to work.

Evolution

It begins with the electronic screams
coming from the alarm clock
the creation of the universe

prime the coffee maker
do the obligatory shower
for everyone's noses
make lunches
and let the dogs out to piss

osmosis through my front door
and amoeba my way
down the block

the old retired couple
who sit on their front porch
drinking java
greet me first
send out their border collie

the dog presents me with a soft Frisbee
I UFO it across their lawn
and Rover flies like Michael Jordan

they wish me a good day

Anything can be Verbed

with my knuckles dragging on the ground
I Neanderthal along
I see a man
on an electric scooter
being lifted by an electronic forklift
into a Para Transpo van
and feel Darwin's ghost give me a shove

I see a mother and her child
walking to daycare
        my spine straightens

I enter my shopping mall
and see a poster of a woman
in the window of La Senza
wearing less than a loincloth

I find the door to the stairs
which leads skyward
to my office floor

when I arrive at my desk
I turn on my computer
and punch the keys of logic

I am the modern man.

Poor Visibility

I can hear a jet in the sky
but cannot see it

the ether
a piece of Italian marble
blue sky veins coursing
through its façade

I watched a reality show
last night with my wife
a fellow told a story
about how his father had
left him
at thirteen
returned at twenty
he said he had forgotten
what his father had looked like

I wonder
if I were to die today
how long it would be
before my young kids
would forget my face?

my father has been in the ground
twenty years now

<u>I can hear him</u>
<u>I have difficulty seeing him</u>
like that jet in the sky.

I only remember his laugh. I can't remember what our conversations sound like. He cannot help me talk through all the problems a girl would go to her dad for. But he's laughing with me in the good times and I can feel his hug whenever I need him.

Adolescent lawn
robins squeeze and pick worms
flowers about to pop.

In Good Order

Rain
an accident waiting to happen
the clouds
a bruised and swollen foot

the repetition of my walk
producing the illusion
of order

entering the shopping centre
the notes of Michael Jackson's
Billy Jean play
over the mall's speakers

I wonder if the security guards
are having a good laugh
watching me on closed circuit
as I sashay down the hall
    stop, spin on my toe
    slide sideways
    moonwalk

chaos
within repetitious order

white mannequins

stare at me like Buddhist statues
I breakdance by them
to let them know
that the kid
is not my son

in the basement
a man with pepper spray
and a walkie
strapped to his belt
snickers.

Circles

The sky is
the black canopy
of my umbrella

my focus is
d
o
w
n

the puddles
dance with circles
Jurassic Park dinosaur ripples
in a glass

their lives
a quarter of a second
      a double ring
        then gone

millions of drops fall around me

the lucky ones
get to make a splash

the other ones

just make everything else
wet.

Machine Gun

Why does America hate itself?
that's what I was thinking about
when I came across
a stick lying on the ground

it looked like
a machine gun

a kid could grab it
put it under his arm
and go
"rat tat tat tat tat »

not even a squirrel
would die
here
in Canada
but he might play
possum.

Shameful

Under an oyster shell
the sky bleached
by a thin layer of clouds
I walk behind a man with headphones
            behind a man who doesn't know
I'm there
because he is a man with headphones

and an attractive girl
with tight jeans
goes surfing by on her skateboard

the man turns his head to glare

he sees me behind him
and quickly turns away
embarrassed to be staring
at such a young girl

I turn my head
nobody's behind me
and I stare
shamefully
at her perfect
ass
rolling away.

Comic Relief

Today I'm the clown
and the weather
is the cold wet cream pie

it smacks me in the face
as soon as I walk out
the front door

as I walk to work in the rain
my right shoe
comically squeaks like a dog toy
with each
and every step

an ocean wave of wind
comes hurtling down
then reverses back up
in speedboat style
inverting my umbrella
like an aquatic creature
flapping its wings

I fight with my parasol
with Chaplin panache
eventually regaining composure
but not dignity

I manage to arrive
at my building
but not before my umbrella
closes over my head
around my face
like a Venus fly trap

I am a new superhero
Umbrellahead-Man

I am the fool.

My giant shadow
fortune-teller prediction
future looks sunny.

Spring Sprung

The day reeks of possibilities
the stench of Dale Carnegie
wafts through the air
and I want to ring everyone's doorbell
after I have snuck copies of Tony Robbins
and Deepak Chopra
and Oprah Winfrey
into their mailboxes

look up
look up
there is nothing but pies
and golden rings
and silver linings
and magic carpets
and pink elephants
and hot air balloons

I want to follow the money trail
I want to believe in the advertising
I want to just do it
in my running shoes
I want to run up to strangers
and tell them
that this is the first day
of the rest of their lives

and it's chock-full of potential
chock-full of hope
and love
and people off their meds
and manic wonder

this is the power of Spring
this is the face of God
and she is barfing up
lilacs and tulips
and crocuses
and the greenest supple leaves
all over the bursting landscape

run through it with me
like the Merry Pranksters
like Prefontaine
like Usain Bolt

come away with me
dear reader
hold my hand
as we walk to work together
as we skip like children
in our rain boots
picking up fat worms
off the sidewalk
and tossing them

to the fat robins
in the dew-soaked grass

come with me
waltz out of this season
dance away from innocence

come hopscotch
come double-dutch
come all thee faithful

come away with me

I promise not to embarrass you
say goodbye a block before
we get there

I promise you this will be fun
I promise you will have
no regrets
I promise you no such thing
as no such thing

hurry now
catch up silly
for this is an adventure of a lifetime
building it one letter
one word

one poem
at a time

take my hand
and come away with me
bring your youth
and your sexy jeans
and your white teeth
and your enthusiasm
for we are about to run
full tilt
into the beckoning arms
of Summer.

SUMMER

an empty beer can in the park

The First Day of Summer

This is the fairgrounds
the hole through the fence
the blue candyfloss tongue
and the close-your-eyes spin

this is where we run and hide
under the bleachers
with a six-pack of beer
and a mickey of Southern Comfort

this is where
she pulls out her gum
and pops it back in after
we have finished

after
under the shirt
under the bra
and down the pants

we leave the empties behind
light cigarettes
and try to win a stuffed bear

the world is opening up
this season verging

on adulthood

but not yet
not so serious yet
summer vacation
nobody is getting old
on summer vacation
nobody is thinking about the future
nobody is thinking about what is coming next

this is the top of the first
this the king's pawn sliding out two spaces
this is the leap off the dock
this is the first day of summer.

Engaged with My Surroundings

There is a big fir tree
that wears a large florescent orange
Frisbee ring
halfway up its trunk
        the ring hanging off the end of a branch
like the tree was showing off
a big fat engagement ring
like it had married the earth

sad children
wait for the divorce
at the pawn shop.

War Machine

Today is not a walk
today is a march
a mindless army march
a bloody hell of a march
a screaming Sergeant
where the weight of world is carried
in a great green army pack
upon my shoulders

and that Sergeant screams
and screams
and screams
a-left
a-left
a-left-right-left

a-left
a-left
a-left-right-left

and each
step is worse
than the last
and my mind has gone numb
to the din
of the tin drum

that beats with relentless cruelty

this isn't about a paycheque
it's only about the numb rub
of a military march
and each step
turning me into a machine
a killing machine

I spit
hating the earth
hating humanity
as my feet carry me along

reaching the mall
a little old lady appears
and I hold the door open for her
and she is surprised
and false teeth appear
plastic bullets
they shoot and kill me

she is delighted
that someone in this day and age
    would hold the door for her
and she says thank you
and to my surprise
I tell her she is welcome

and just like that
involuntarily
my humanity returns
as a soldier dies
in the deep trenches
of a shopping mall.

The Garden

For years
I've been walking by it
the house with the ugly garden

I don't think
you could even call it that

it looks like a pile
of dark earth
six feet long
four feet wide
two feet tall

the man who lives there
has placed big grey ugly rocks
spaced every few feet apart
around its oval circumference

in the centre
three grey cement planters
sprout spiky plants
and blood-red flowers

I see the old man
sometimes
when I walk home

out there weeding
his mound of earth
weeding his ugly garden

I pass by it
and wonder
why have I never
seen his wife?

Dress Code

There is a spot
on the street
across from the church
where federal employees
park their cars
so they don't get
tickets
from the mall cops

a man gets out
of his car

he is wearing a grey dress shirt
tucked into black capris
with a white belt
and he is wearing white shoes
with white socks
pulled as high as the cliffs of Dover
and this allows
two inches
of calf flesh
access to the sun

he walks with determination
and with the pride of a man
who has outsmarted

the parking authority

I follow him to the mall
where we both work

in my heart
I know
he lives like Dracula

without mirrors.

The secret menu
ambulance at McDonald's
heart-attack special.

The Shoe

A man's left shoe
        black
        leather
        laces tied

a dress shoe
        elegant
        square-toed
        slightly worn
        polished
        maintained

a shoe for
a wedding
a funeral
a business venture

at the intersection
by the crosswalk button
like the man had just
                vanished
alien abduction
teleported
time-travelled
the unnoticed
        fall out of the gym bag

maybe a surrealist
is afoot

maybe the bachelor party
got out of hand

the next day
it walked away
all by itself.

An Ocean of Sky

Last night I watched TV
I saw you
fighting for your freedom
in your own country
and I saw you
starving
and crying
and living hard
in different countries
around the world

and there you were again
my human brother
my human sister
raped and killed
in some foreign land

not today
this morning
I take you
by the hand
smile like children do
and jump together
into the pale blue ocean
of the sky we both
share

we swim out deep
until we can no longer hear
the screams of gunfire

we float on our backs
holding hands
smiling

and then suddenly I realize
you aren't there
by my side

and then suddenly I remember
the world is cruel.

Weeds

Thinking clouded
by all the chores
that need to be done

I pass by the house
where the young man
with Down Syndrome lives

the lawn is all weeds
not a stitch of grass
just clumps and clumps
of weeds
so big they resemble
science fiction plants
of a desert world

sometimes coming home
from work
I see the boy
on garbage day
lugging his recycle bins
around the corner
to his garage
with the dilapidated paint job
like it was scorched by acid

then a driver
not looking
or not caring
or both
almost runs me down
at the light

after the "Hey whatthefuck dude!"
SNAP
I am brought to thoughts of my own mortality

what I need to be doing
switches to
what I didn't do

hospital wards engulf my head
as I continue
to walk

I see the first hot air balloon
of the year
flying high

I've never been in one

what needs to be done

needs
weeds.

Steamy Hot Flesh

The humidity
has made perspiration
useless
static moisture rests
on my brow and forearms
as I do my Dr. Livingston shuffle

the leaves of the trees
are out of puberty
now youthfully supple
strong and gorgeous
their vitality
an intoxication to behold

Alice Cooper
has let out the human children
has dated me and
made me feel my age

and there they are
at the bus stop
with their heads bowed
to their electronic gods
the young girls
and boys
littering the summer

with their flesh

the varicose vein in my leg
looks at me
and smiles cruelly.

Empty tree branch waits
yellow school bus vanishes
tire swing appears.

As the Ash Trees Die

I walk
amongst confused seasons

I walk
along Kilborn Avenue
through flavours of time

I walk
where the city has marked
the Emerald Ash trees
with red Xs
across their bellies

the Emerald Ash trees
look like they are
in the wrong season
look like they are in autumn
look like they have been through
chemotherapy
they lost all their leaves
      to a killer bug

and across the street
it's winter
the Japanese lilacs
have fully bloomed

their white cone-shaped flowers
cover their own branches
like thick heavy snow
so beautiful
their scent
        so lovely

I breathe in their perfume
and feel so alive

I walk
as all around me
the Ash trees
        so die.

Walking to Work with My Dead Friend

He was my friend
we grew up together
he wanted to be a writer
his vocabulary was twice mine now
and he died seventeen years ago

he might have been
manic-depressive
but like most
when they are manic
they are
crazy-clown pop-up-box fun
Van Gogh brilliant

he was that
and more

when I walk to work
I often think about him
often harness his joy
and energy for language
for life
I try to take it and let it flow
through me
my hands
needles

ink these tattoo-words on the white page
like they would be read here forever
he's knocking on everyone's doors
pulling people out of bed
stuffing cigars into their mouths
putting drinks in their hands
putting paper party hats on their heads

now the neighbourhood
is doing a drunk conga line down
the middle of the road
my dead friend leading the way

I'm still on the sidewalk
watching
when he is now back
beside me
jumping
up and down
poking me in the chest
making fun of me
for being so conservative
for missing all the beauty
in this very second
for missing this party

now on my walk
I'm *so-o-o-o-o* bloody alive

being told off
by my dead friend

I shoot his junky spirit energy
into my arm
and type these words
with the speed and ecstasy
of a religious zealot

I'm performing it
I'm living it
I'm doing it
a roundhouse
a backflip
a somersault

I'm sky-diving

I fall from the expansive blue sky
land on the sidewalk
like Ironman
and take a bow

I walk to work
with a grin,
my dead friend
running ahead of me
telling me to hurry
the fuck up.

Thought for Food

Marshmallow meringue clouds
stuffed with blueberry ether
resting in the Earth's warm crust

dessert at seven a.m.
my brain eats the sky

I digest it
all day.

Empty rum mickey
sidewalk church intersection
devil sleeps it off.

Heat Wave

The whole atmosphere
has too much saliva
in its mouth

the trees sag full
as the air conditioners
threaten mutiny
and the dogs are
too hot
to bark

everything is a swimming pool
left to rot

I'm a swamp creature
sliming in the green algae

the weather is supposed to
break
next week

if I make it
I'll be hot sludge
crossing the finish line

my neighbours are all outside

cooking breakfast
on their asphalt
driveways

my balls have silly-puttied
to mid-calf
and my mind
has turned to popsicles
walk-in freezers
and igloos
as I listen to bacon
and eggs
sizzle
as I slide down the street

I am melting butter

when I arrive
at my air-conditioned mall
I pour myself
through the door
and God hits my body
with a heavy bag of crushed ice

I reform
into a jelly
solidify back to a solid
reconstituted

but my packing is bent
weird

you shouldn't refreeze
poets

I think about the walk home
the breakdown
solid
liquid
vapour

I will rain over the Atlantic
become part of a tuna
become part of a sandwich
become part of someone else
become the fiction
          of some poet's mind
become this poem
on a day
that's
too hot
to make
sense.

Melting Clouds

The clouds are
white candle wax
melting
        the sun
        its burning flame

the humidity
hasn't let up
neither has my distaste
for reality

I marvel at my very short
very finite existence
like somebody opened a door
from a pitch-black room
and showed you everything
and then quickly shut it again

how odd

to be as before
I was born
I will be
the same
again

I marvel at the concept
of "I"
a fiction
degrading in old age
a consciousness loop

my friend can no longer argue
with his mother who has been dipped
in Alzheimer's

where did she go?
her "I"
runny ice-cream

I jam my foot
into the door.

Dick and his dog Spot
tennis ball lies in the grass
too damn hot to fetch.

Pixelating Summer

Like losing a radio station
summer is breaking up
fragmenting around me

a small red leaf corkscrews down
in front of me
pixelating my season

my antenna limbs
swing
and bring nothing into focus

a man at a bus stop on his cellphone
"You're breaking up like crazy"

a truck flies by shifting into the angriest gear

a bus squeaks and spits
groans gas like static pistons whistle

squawky seagulls modulate
dialing in the parking lot
they protest time
the low morning temperature
and the lack of edible garbage

when I arrive at work
this Monday morning
my co-worker informs me
heart attacks occur on Mondays
more than any other day
of the week

the reception is definitely
fuzzy.

What I Didn't Know

Sometimes I think to myself
when I'm in the shower
this could be my last day on earth

I mean who knows
you could be hit by a bus
and that's it

and what I didn't know
as I strolled into work
trying to think of a good poem
trying to think of something to write

what I didn't know
was a bus was going to strike a train
an hour after I arrived
at work

I saw the pictures online
the front of the double-decker bus
sheared off
at least five dead
multiple people injured

a co-worker came into my cubicle
later that morning

and said
"Imagine those people
getting dressed in the morning
and off to work
and that's it"

she didn't know
they didn't know
I didn't know

you never know.

Crows perched on crosses
summertime crucifixion
they caw cold and black.

Equinox

The day
a cold wet corpse

frost on the rooftops
houses
glazed donuts
served at a wake

crows fly through
the death of this season

turning the corner
the expanse of sky
much to my surprise
is greyish pink

the rouge
on the powdered cheeks
of the cadaver

her headstone
        my calendar
her beauty remains in my head
like a Beach Boys song
her smile of hot sun
and the last gurgling sounds

of finishing a soda
with a straw
          (the same suction sounds from
                    the operating room before the flatline)

Summer is dead.

AUTUMN

melancholy music

The young leaf forgets
one day it will be old
and fall to the ground.

All the leaves dying
spectacular colourful
the firs could care less.

God's halitosis
breath of a dying season
stroll through saliva.

My aunt lost her sight
all this orange red now-gone
rage burns in colour.

Dripping faucet sky
paper-towel clouds leak on me
the city sleeps well.

Hendrix plays Dylan
all along the watchtower
melancholy music.

The banana peel
blackening asks the question
comic gold or trash.

My sky a teabag
wet, soggy, left in the mug
soil a dry biscuit.

Iridescent leaf
a sky fish amidst a school
about to swim off.

I walk briskly now
the wind has come with teeth
my zipper smiles shut.

Profound wet sadness
autumn a mental patient
lost without his meds.

A dripping faucet
my sky leaks melancholy
my boots squishing tears.

Mailbox graffiti
immortalized with spray cans
sunshine and rust kill.

Walking through colour
sun evaporates wet leaves
I crunch through dry sound.

The wind carries me
to the dirty parking lot
I rest like street trash.

Industrial boots
stepped in white paint and walked
around the blue sky.

Daylight savings time
back to bed for Dracula –
missed the crimson sky.

Ideas pour out
as I make my way to work
while everything dies.

The grey clouds stab me
the colour from my mind drains
then a crimson leaf.

Colour power-punch
rainbow bloody-nose landscape
pugilist stagger.

A funny tree kicked
on my way to work today
wet leaf to the groin.

A black bare oak branch
a black crow announces death
white snow on the verge.

It is this moment
when dawn kisses the blackness
I touch God's hand.

WINTER

the witch's tit

Liquid Paper

It's like when you go to the store
to get something you really need
and all the way there you plan
and scheme
about what you are going to do
with that thing
once you get it
and you think
isn't it going to be great
and you reach for the door handle
and pull
      astonishment
      disbelief
      dismay

it's locked

your eyes come straight ahead
and you read the red sign

      CLOSED

that's what it was like
when the first big snowfall happened
no chance of going back
the snow

like a bureaucratic giant with liquid paper the
size of the Peace Tower
painting everything pure clean white
censoring out the phonography of spring
summer and autumn

little stickler
missed the tit
of the witch.

The Snow

For the children
it's glittering magic which lines the tiniest tree branch
icing sugar
love

for the addict
it's a fantasy land
of lines to be snorted

for *Campbell's*
it's an ad for reduced sodium levels

for darkness
it's genocide

for snowmen
it's terraforming

for the ski shop
it's uphill profit

for the wife of the plow operator
it means waking up
in an empty bed

for the writer

it's the empty page

for the Canadian
it's defining

for the Hollywood producer
it's a science fiction set piece

for the homeless
it's a bitch

for the priest
it's more proof
for the existence of God

for the scientist
it's just H_2O.

Dominatrix

The sky has gone
all fifty shades of grey
and Winter has taken off
the clean white dress
of the girl next door
and slipped on
her black leather miniskirt

the cold spray
of an open trawler
fishnets

she stands topless
with cruelty in her heart
the wind her whip

the forecast says she
will be back to normal
by the end of the week

but for now
she raises her arm high

she strikes me
and
I shudder.

Mr. Saggy Balls and Ms. Suicide

My sky is flat white
my sky isn't my sky
my sky is my ceiling
I'm lying
in bed
at home
sick
feeling like I did
twenty-five years ago
when I had mono

today my walk
is only in my mind
back in time
when my temperature spiked
to 107
and they called an ambulance for me

I ended up in Emerg
lying next to a young woman
who failed to kill herself with pills

on the other side of the room
was a pile-up of car crash victims
covered in bandages

the prettiest intern I ever saw
came and checked me over
head-to-toe
even pulled down my underwear
and gazed curious at my limp cock
and saggy balls

I answered her questions
as Ms. Suicide gently wept
in the next bed

the pretty intern finished
smiled and walked away

as my enthusiasm followed her
so happy to be alive.

Cold Jazz

It's like I'm looking out
of the asshole of a wolf
the circumference
of my oval view
encrusted white fur
condensation from my own breath

when I breathe
a cloud of steam appears
for an instant
and then vanishes
like a dragon
who is sleeping

I'm wearing long underwear
and a coat which can
hold me in a loving embrace
until -40 Celsius
and then after that
who gives a shit

when I blink
my eyelashes
stick together
like they were covered
in syrup

ahead of me
is a bus stop
there is a large poster
of Diana Krall

she is almost life-size
her beautiful blonde hair
blowing behind her head
like seaweed in a tide

I walk past her on tour
as she holds a note
into her microphone
frozen.

Bitch Slapping the Sky

The sky is a bruise
the moon a glittering earring
and winter is a pimp
keeping his whore
of an atmosphere
in line.

It Keeps Him Out of Trouble

My neighbour is in the army
not sure what he does for them

sometimes I see him
in his green relish outfit
coming or going
to or from
work

other times I tell him
I can't see him
when he's in his
green relish suit
        never heard that one before

he has done a couple of tours
in Afghanistan
I remember seeing him
after he had just gotten back from one

he was focusing on his front walkway
the beautiful stairs and deck
he had built himself before he left

I don't know what he does for the army

I don't ask
he doesn't say

I saw him this morning clearing the snow
    off his truck
as I headed
    off to work

I saw him on the weekend
shovelling the snow on his driveway
even though he has a paid service to do it

hours later he was working on it again
I asked him why
when he has a paid service to do it
he answered
    it keeps him out of trouble

I think about that now on the walk to work

it keeps him out of trouble

everything that implies
    after two tours of duty.

Extra Christmas lights
electrical meter burns
house aflame in colour.

The Existential Quandary of Rudolph

The street
is all Jack-the-Ripper
fog so thick
the street lights look like
floating lanterns in the sky

but then the blow-up Christmas decorations
on the lawns of the houses
turn it all Frosty the Snowman
strangling the nightmare sensibility
of the weather
with a string of coloured lights

giving Rudolph
reason
purpose
pride

wish it did the same for me

the cold wind
doesn't turn my nose red
merely
light pink.

The Two Christmas Trees of Kilborn Avenue

There are two Christmas trees
I pass every day in the month of December
on my way to work
and most of January too
on my way to work

they are big firs
towering
with twinkling coloured lights
beacons of love and hope

their owners must have used a hoist
to get the lights all the way
up there

these trees are so beautiful
they soften my atheist soul
as I strap baby Jesus
into the carrier on my chest
and together we walk

along the way
we pick up the homeless
and the poor
and the sick
and the dying

and those who were forgotten
and those who were left behind
and those fell
and needed a hand up

yes, me and baby J
we carry them all
in the radiance
of the two Christmas trees of Kilborn Avenue
and for just a moment
I feel the love of God
and the desire to help
everyone
do everything that's right
              and just

that's what happens
whenever
I walk past
the warm glow
of the two Christmas trees
of Kilborn Avenue.

Winter's Bony Hand

It is here
in the pitch black
of this winter's morning
when Death grips
my insulated glove
with his bony hand
      and sends a chill up my spine
and we walk
together like children
my teeth chattering the whole way
him chattering about
what a busy season he is having

he leaves me at my workplace
to find a homeless man
in -40 Celsius
sleeping on the street
somebody
to curl up with

inside the warmth of my building
I unwrap myself like the Invisible Man
wondering
if Mr. Bony will show up
for my walk home

pretty sure
he'll catch me by surprise.

Lean Cuisine wrapper
Fettuccine Alfredo-
embedded snowbank.

I Paint the City's Dreams

This morning I walk
in the subconscious glow
of the city's dreams

the streets are glazed
like candy
and I navigate them
like a comedic silent film star

and here we are
in this repetition
this endless
            taking out the garbage
            changing the light bulb
            doing the dishes

to this walking-to-work
repetition
I scream
in my best villain voice
"You'll never take me alive!"

and here and now
we make something
from nothing
and march defiantly

(careful you don't slip)
against the banal
against the droning din
of humanity's daily grind

I paint the city's dreams
with Dayglo rainbows
with underground raver visions
with acid-head splatter
with stoned monkeys' ideas of God

I project old science fiction films
on the walls
and put fusion jazz on the surround sound

I pull the ripcord on the *Theremin*
and dance the electric mambo
while lighting the candles, incense, and the load
this is how I
walk to work

art is a product of misery
a tool of coping
a way of understanding
ourselves and our plight

this morning I walk
in the subconscious glow

of the city's dreams

this morning
I very calmly
walk to work.

Walking in the Aftermath

The sky is so grey and boring
its description ran away
        it got tired of running
        sat down
        and waited for a bus
        that never came

the snow is spread out
all over the street
like the aftermath
of a party

Frosty the Snowman
(whipped cream
sliding off of a sundae)
looks half-sloshed

a piece of gift wrap
blows down the road
landing and turning
a hubcap into a present

there is Jesus
on the street corner
with a shovel
cleaning up

and the Christmas trees
are lying in the snowbanks
their childhood joy
sucked out of them
their chlorophyll
mostly still intact

the season
no longer
jolly.

Snow eats consciousness
too cold to think anything
writer ice blockage

Bedside Table

The snow twinkles
sparkles
like Tinkerbell's ass

a person
has left out
a bedside table
at the end of his laneway
with a paper note
taped to its side
      "Free"

the drawer is open
like a kid
trying to catch snowflakes
with her tongue

this winter
is filling our collective consciousness
every mental crack
      like the drawer
with snow

two days later
the sidewalk
looks like it has been murdered

satanic boot rituals
the vomit of a snow plow
and the frozen blood of car exhaust

the moon is a bright white marble
half of it gone
just like
the bedside table.

Ken Goes Surfing

To widen the streets
the plow removed
a good hunk of snow
and now these banks look like
frozen rip tides

I think about getting a Ken doll
and sticking him
on a surfboard
inside the frozen wave
the proportions working well

a fantasy vernissage
in a prestigious art gallery
        "Ken Goes Surfing"
people standing around
grabbing their chins
nodding

but I don't have a camera
and I don't think many people
would appreciate it
anyway.

I Flew Up in the Air and Landed on my Ass

When you find yourself
looking at your boot
like the painter looks at his thumb
you realize
you are the magic act
the one where the magician
has pulled the last sword
away from your back
the sword that was floating you
       in the air
the only thing holding you up
and now you're
a photograph
of a tossed Frisbee
flat   parallel to the earth   suspended
you're the banana peel cartoon

you're the freeze-frame of the high jumper
       going over the bar

and whatever thought you had
is gone
because of ice and angles
and evolution getting us on our own two feet
instead of four on the floor

and your brain has gone code red
and your muscles in your neck
are pulling tight
keeping your head from smacking

you hit the ground
like you were tackled
by some invisible linebacker
and you feel the age
of no-spring-chicken

you get up
shake off the universe's laughter
just like you do
every morning
to carry on.

The Escape Artist

Every day I walk to my cell
where I'm a prisoner
for eight hours

every day
on the way to work
I escape.

Acknowledgments

Some of the poems in this collection have
appeared in some form in Bywords.ca and
In/Words Magazine.

To all the people who take the time to read what
I have written, thank you. It doesn't work without you.

There are some special people I much mention.

I would like to thank my regular readers, Lisa Gregoire,
Jeff Hodgson, Nicole Hillmer, Ross Buskard, and
Michael Dennis.

My mother, Judith Gustafsson, for everything she does
to enable my writing to take place.

Graham O'Neil and Claire McLaughlin for their
constant support.

James and Megan Cantellow, for showing up every time.

Morgan Gay, thanks for reading and re-reading.

Bob Godwin, who taught me about poetry in the first
place.

A very special thanks to Michael Joyal for his beautiful
artwork. Lovely.

Karen Kilby and Vince Jessen (the man who walks the other way) – thanks.

Jason Mutch and Jennifer Baker – lots of love.

Rob James White – to the button.

To my publisher, Matt Joudrey, thank you for taking a chance on an old war horse like me.

To my wonderful editor, Karen Clavelle. Thank you for all your suggestions and hard work. I can't thank you enough.

And finally, to my wife, Marty Carr, who puts up with all my crap, and our wonderful kids, Molly and Henry – I write all this stuff for you. Don't be mad. Love you to bits.